Published by Creative Space 10/31/15

ISBN 13: 978-1517012021
ISBN 10: 1517012023

W, G, A, W, REG, # 1782143 date 05/13/15

Dedicated to my Granddaughter Maeve

I want to thank Min & Jayne

For your help on my book

Love Marty

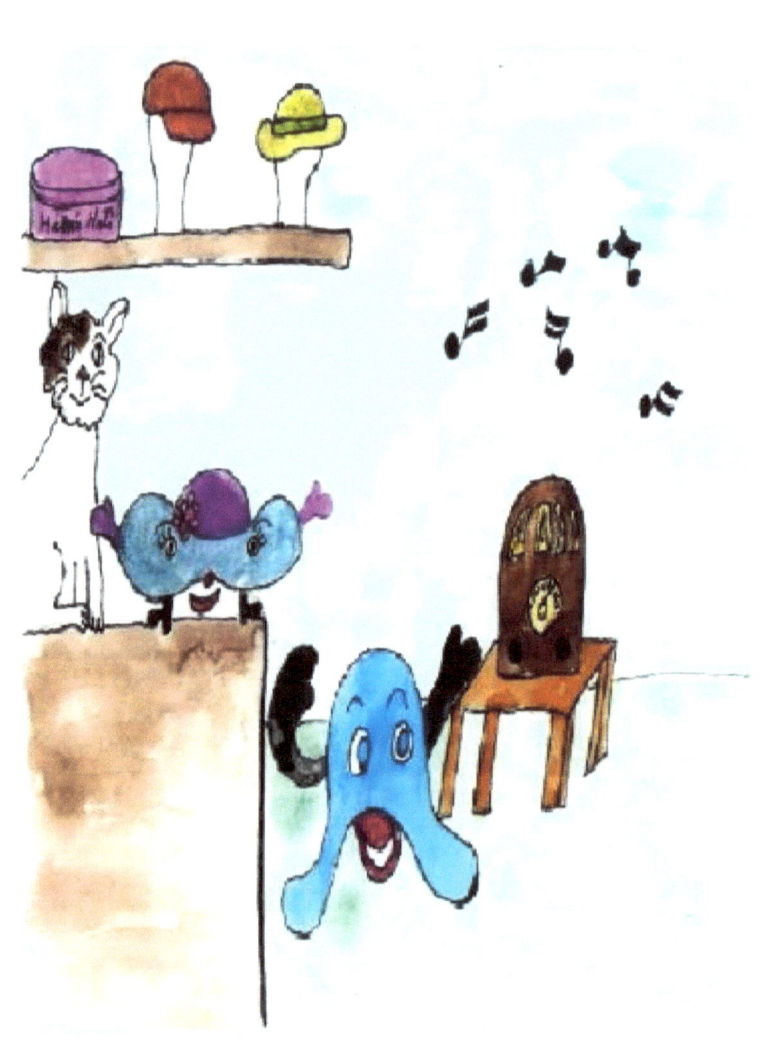

It was a long time since

Mrs. Hubbard was in the shop.

Miss. Cloche was listing to the music

In the shop and dancing.

Mary the cat was sitting on the counter.

Looking at one of the new Hats.

The new hat said what is that hat doing?

She dose that most of the time.

When Helen is not in the shop.

(1)

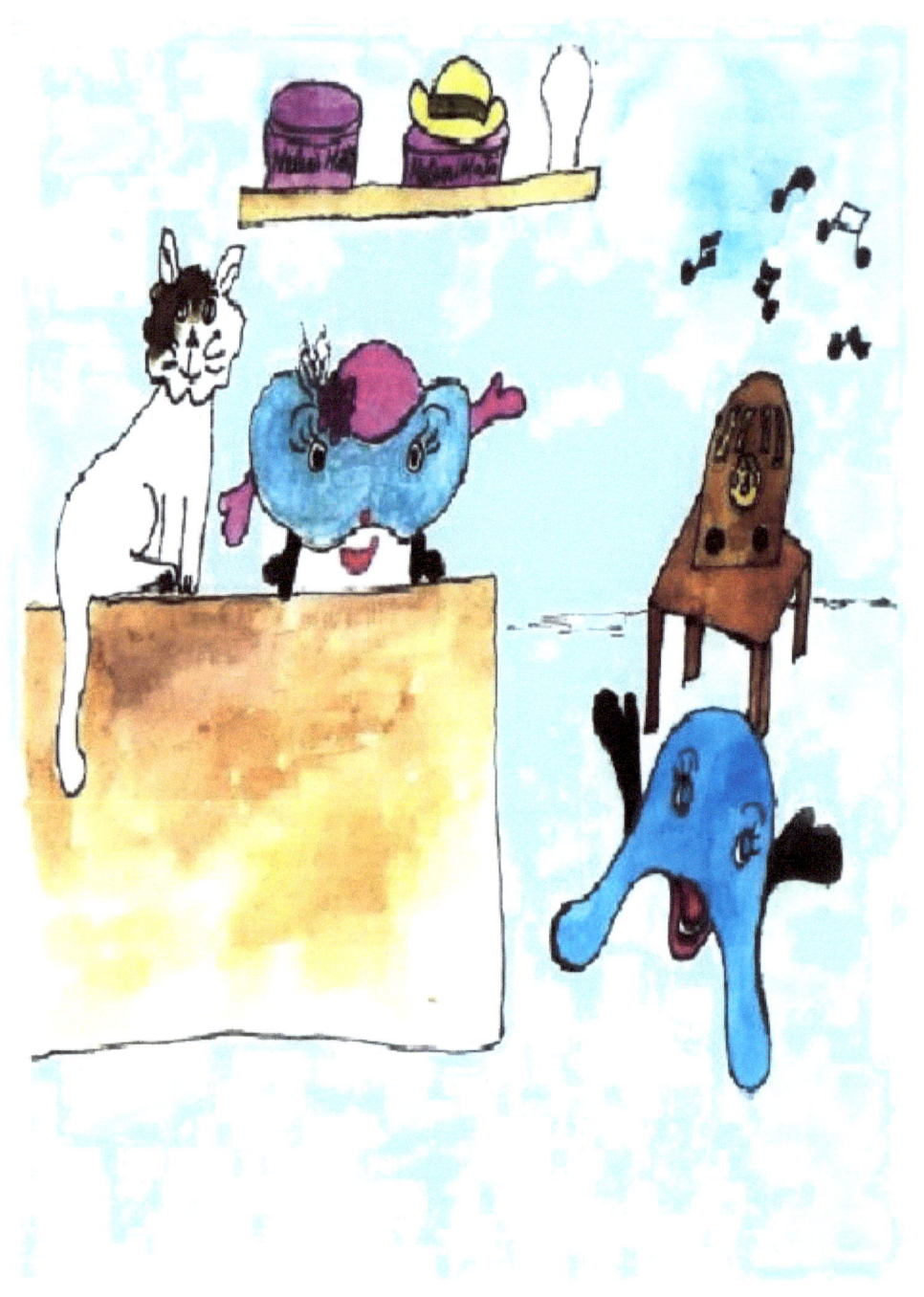

Miss. Cloche said, "To whom are you talking to Mary?"

"One of the new hats Helen has made for

Mrs. Hubbard and her family,"

Miss. Cloche said.

Maybe Mrs. Hubbard will wear

Miss. Pill Box in the next time she come.

Oh, I hope so I miss my friend

Miss. Pill Box so much

(2)

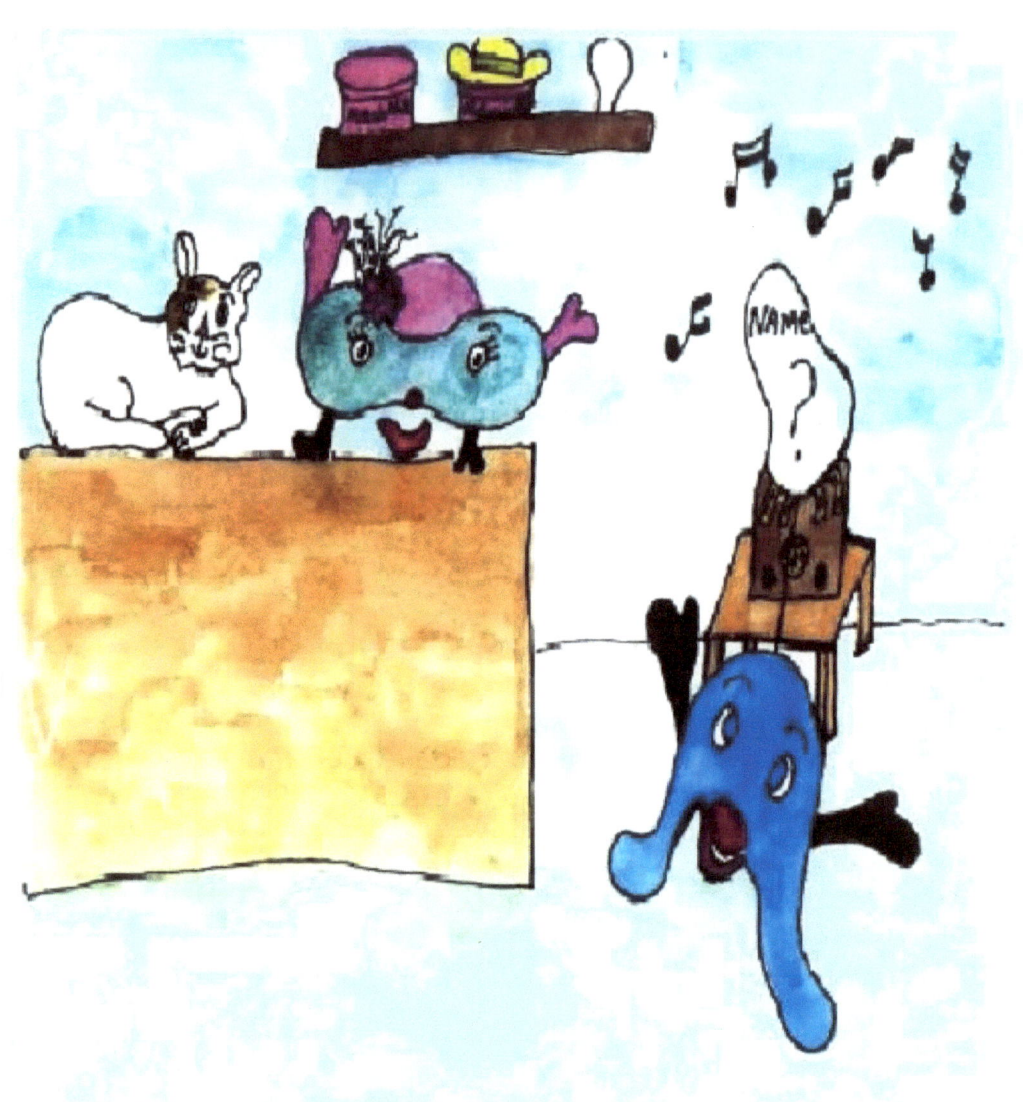

The new hat asked,

"What is a Pill Box?"

Mary Said, "She is a hat

Helen made she used to live here"

"Why does everyone have names?

And not me the new hat asked.

Miss. Cloche said,

"Well we will just have to give you a name"

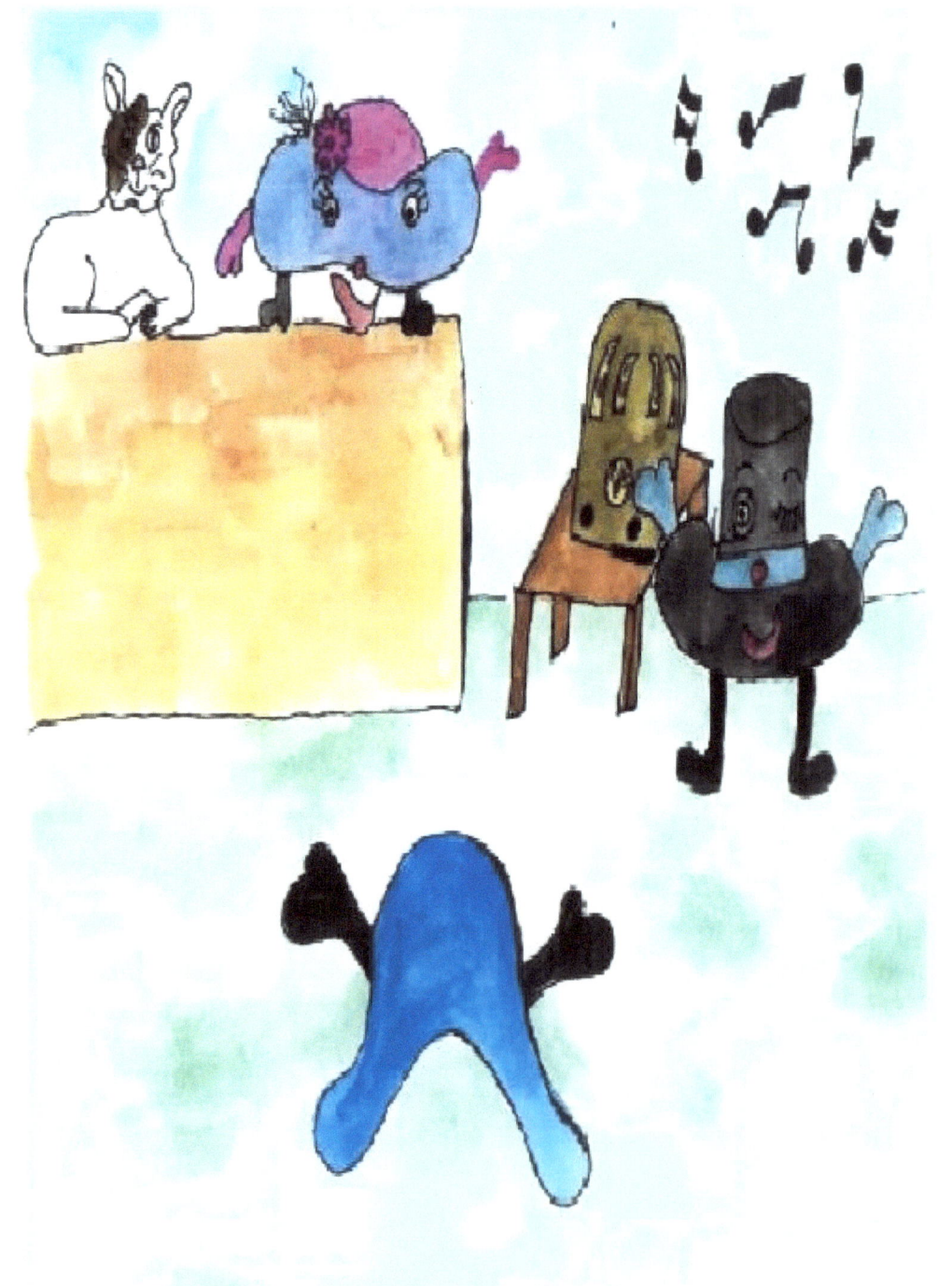

Just then, Mr. Top Hat came by

And said to the new hat,

"Well hello, Missis"

The new hat liked that name, she said.

"That a good name for me"

Mary said, "You're right!

"We well name you Missis," Mr. Top Hat said

That a fine name for a sweets hat like you.

(4)

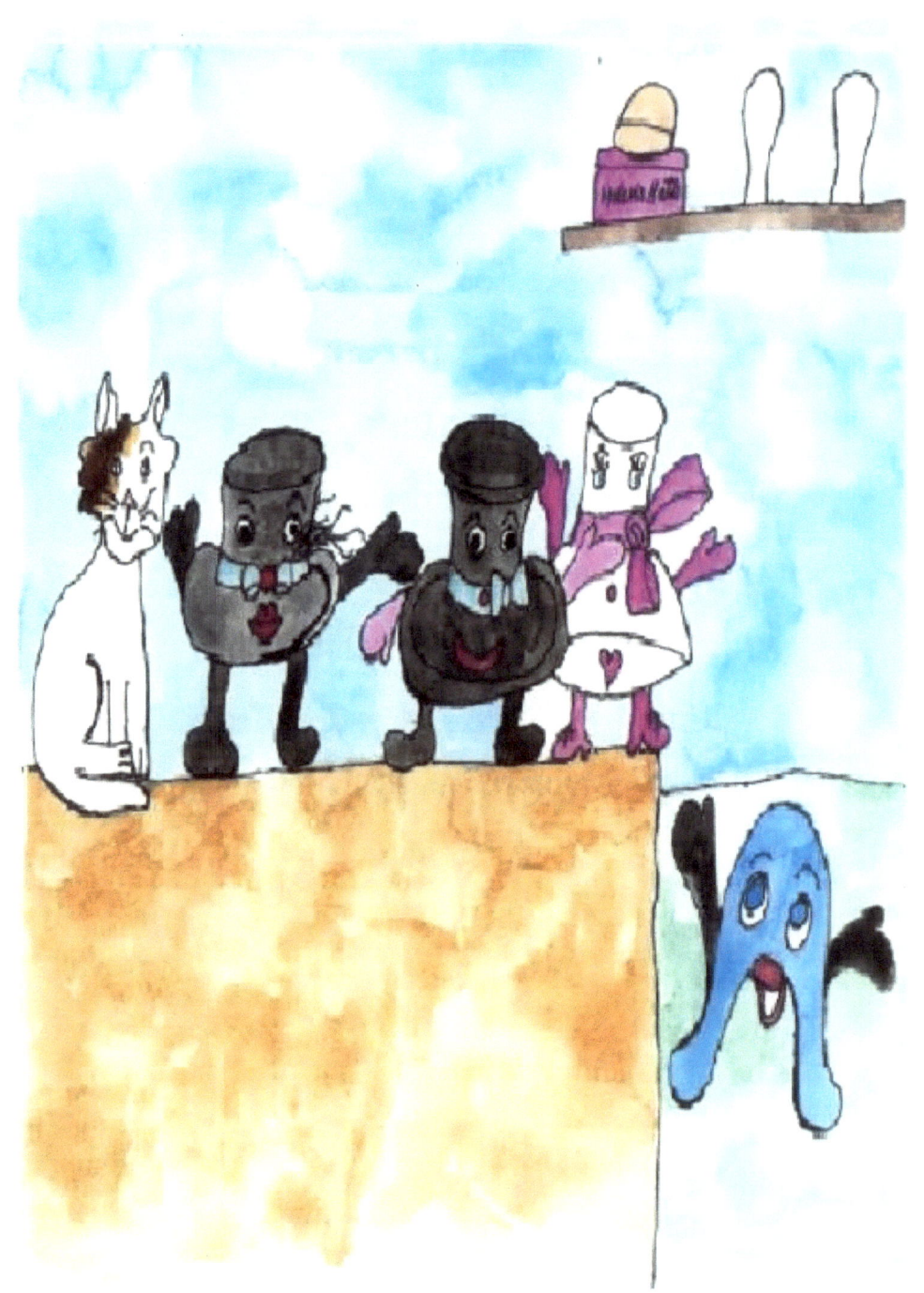

There were three other new hats

On the counter next to Mary the cat.

The new hats said, "We want name too,

Like Missis. "Miss. Cloche said,

"Well let's tack some time and thank about this."

"It is a new project here in the Hat Shop what

Fun it is trying on new name.

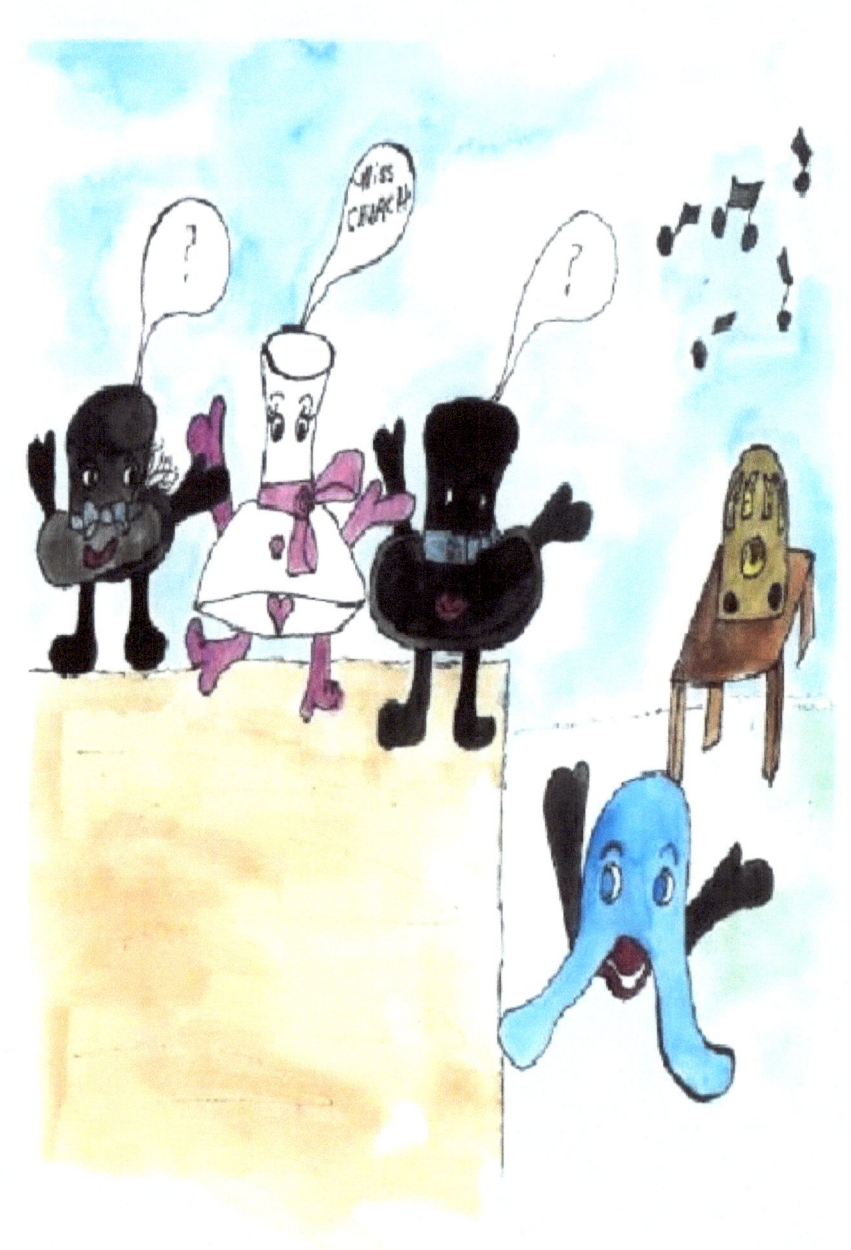

Miss. Cloche was talking to the new hats

And telling them there new names.

Mr. Hamburger, Mr. Jaxon and Miss. Church.

Those where the new name for hats. Miss. Cloche

Had come up with that was there true hat names.

(6)

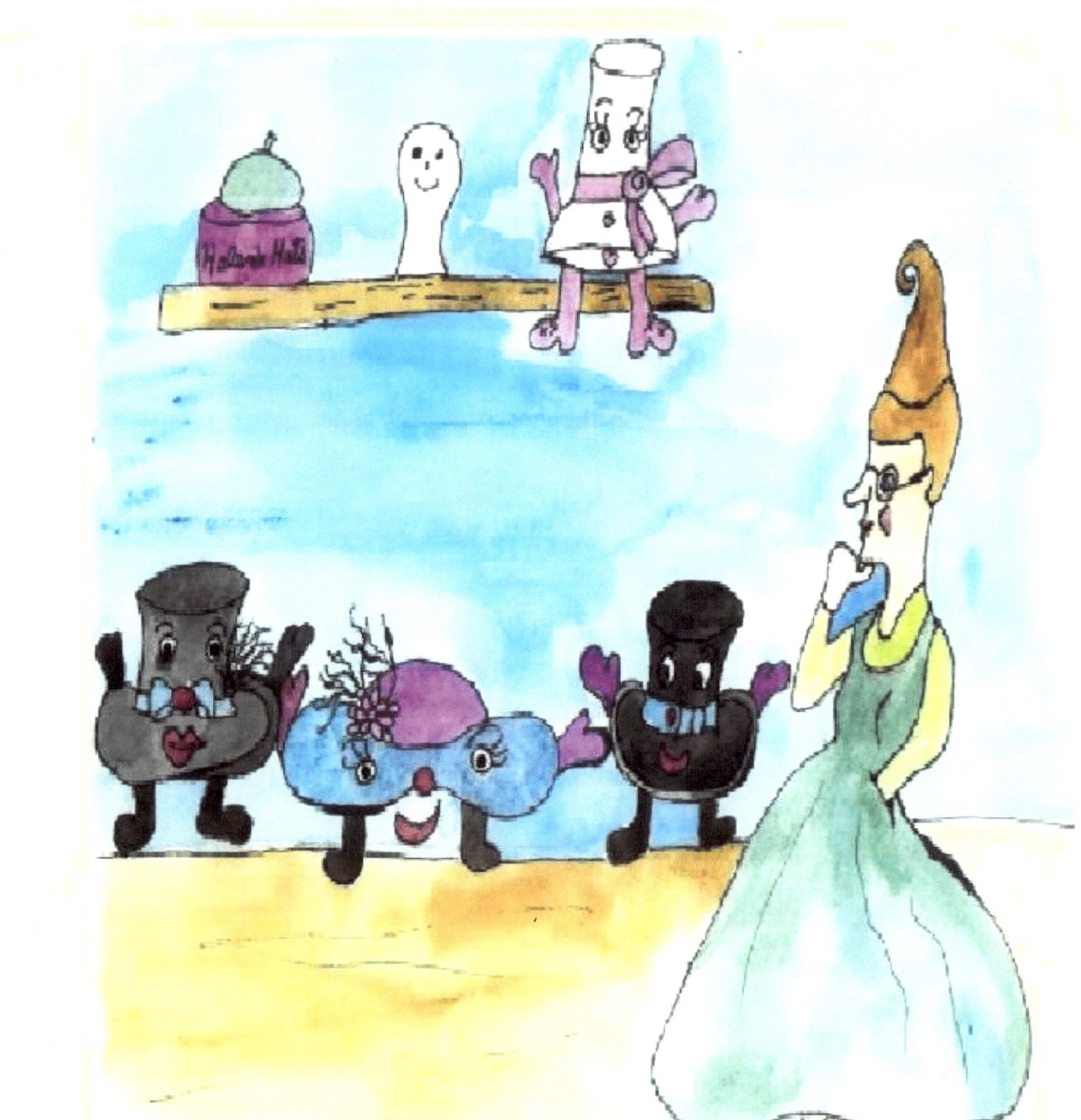

It was time for Helen to come in to the shop.

And start working on the last hat.

It was for Mrs. Hubbard's daughter.

(7)

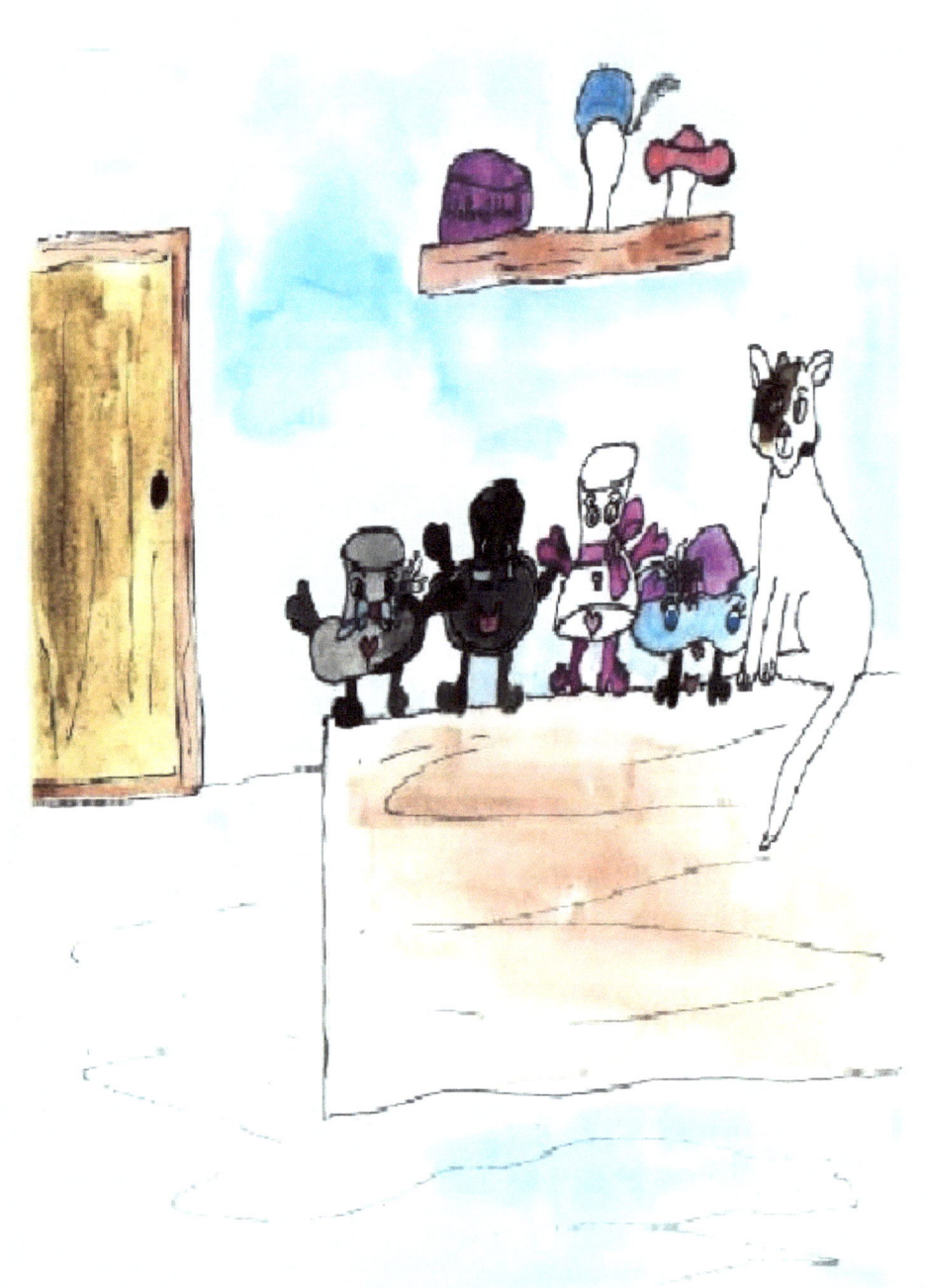

Missis and the other hats asked.

"What is this place?"

Mary said, it is a Hat Shop,

That what you all are hats.

Miss. Helen make hats.

She is called a hatter most of the time.

It is a man why make hats, Helen father was a hatter

And He passed the hat shop on to Helen.

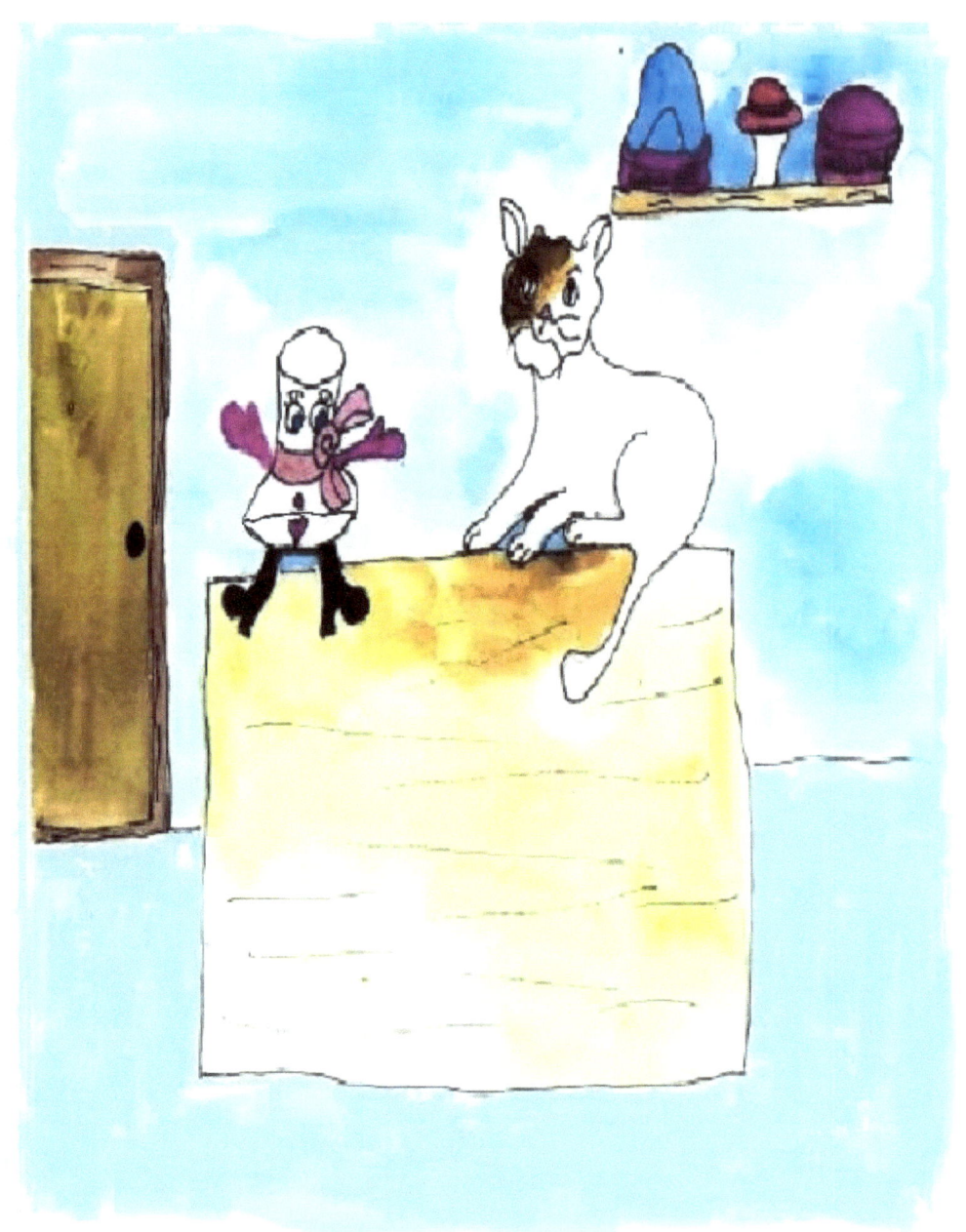

Miss. Church asked, Mary how long

Have you lived in the Hat Shop?

Mary laugh and said, "OH, Oh, a long time my dear."

I can't tell time or day's except when it dinner time.

But I have a lot of fun in the

Hat Shop every day is different.

(9)

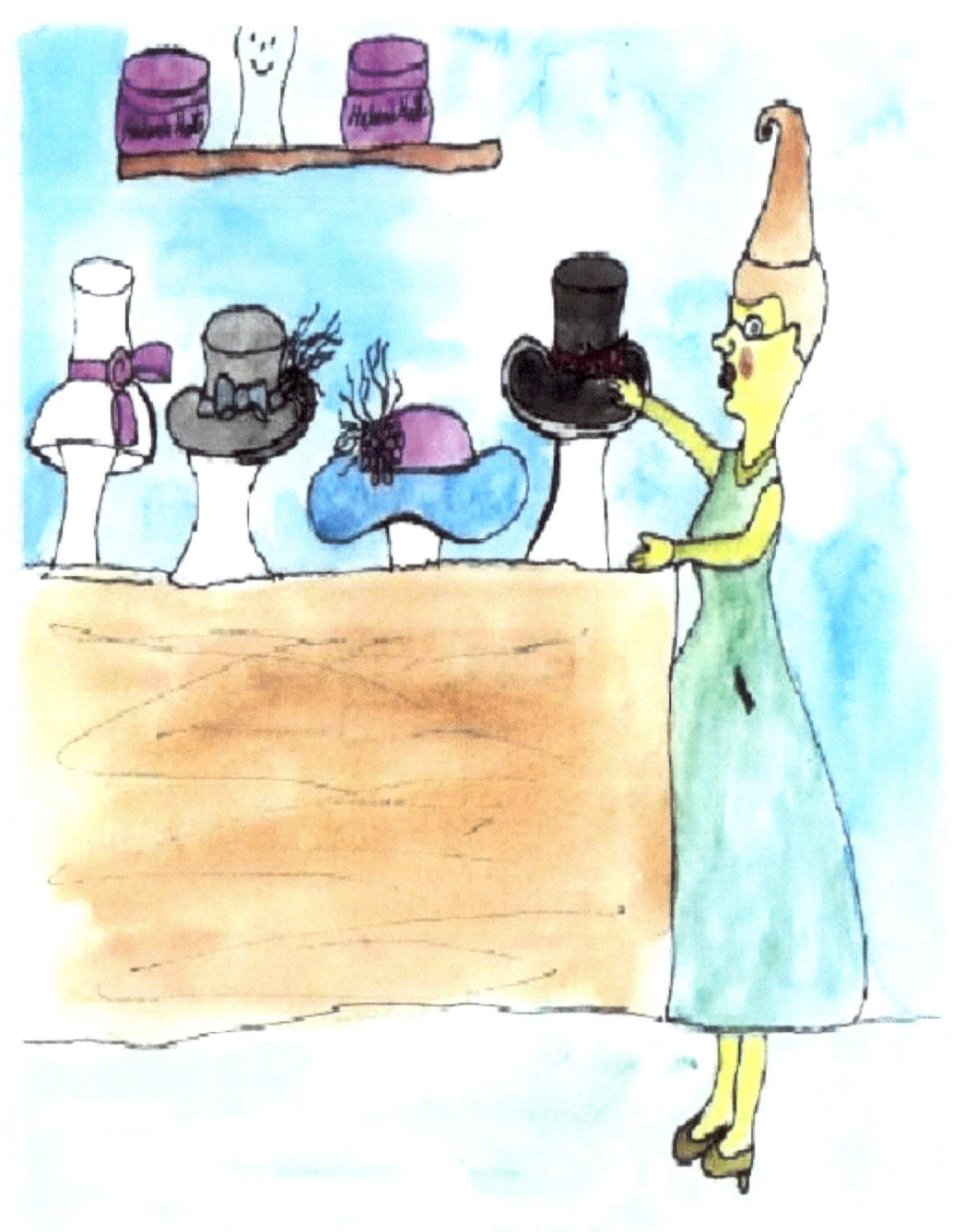

The next day Helen came in early because.

Mrs. Hubbard was going to come in and see

The new hats she had ordered for her family.

To wear to the derby next month

Helen had them all out on the counter.

They all looked so lovely.

Just then, she look at Mr. Jaxon

His hat brim it was a different color!

Helen could not figure this out

This wasn't the first time something

Like this had happened.

It keep happening to the hat in the shop.

(10)

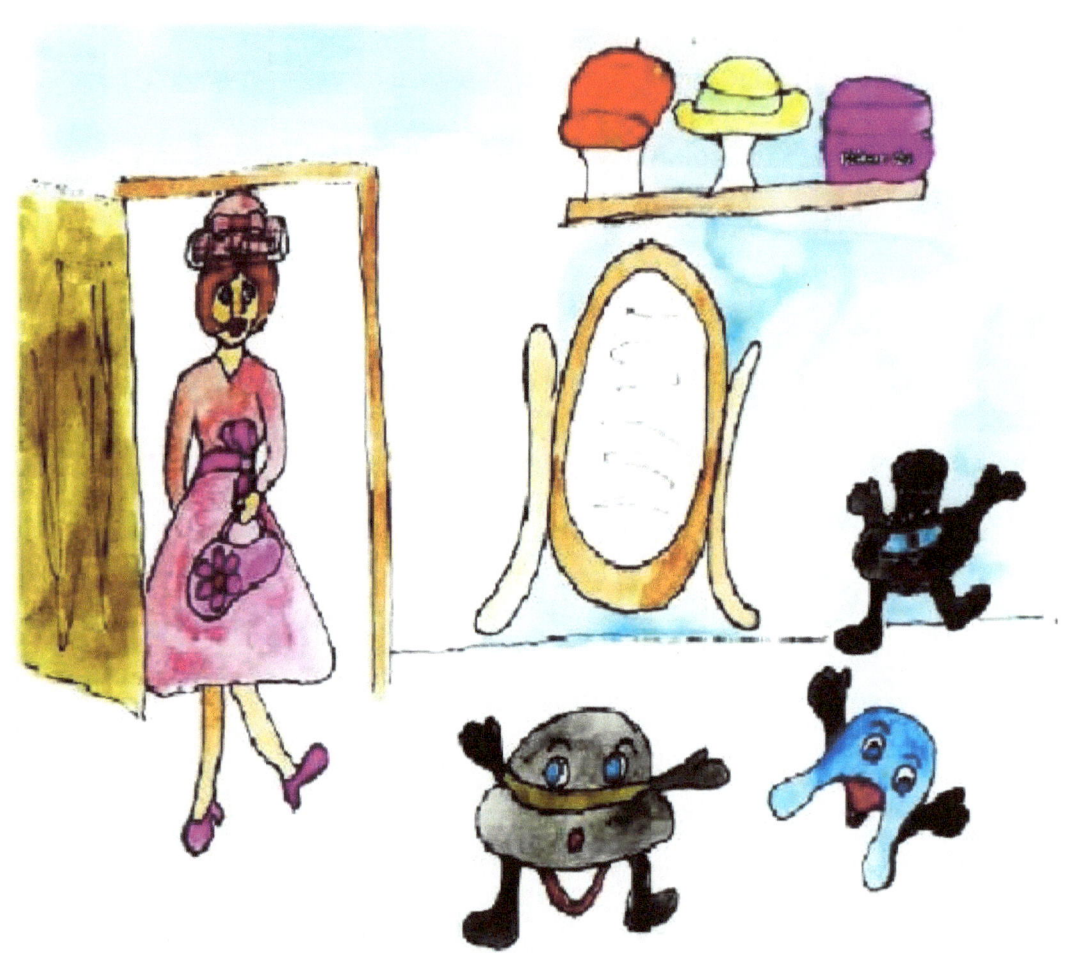

Helen Got Busy fixing the hat before

Mrs. Hubbard came in the shop.

When Mrs. Hubbard came in the

She had Miss. PillBox on.

Mr. Tophat and Mr. Iron hat

were so happy to see her.

Miss. Cloche was too.

They all got togather and were talkintg

And laughting up a storm.

(11)

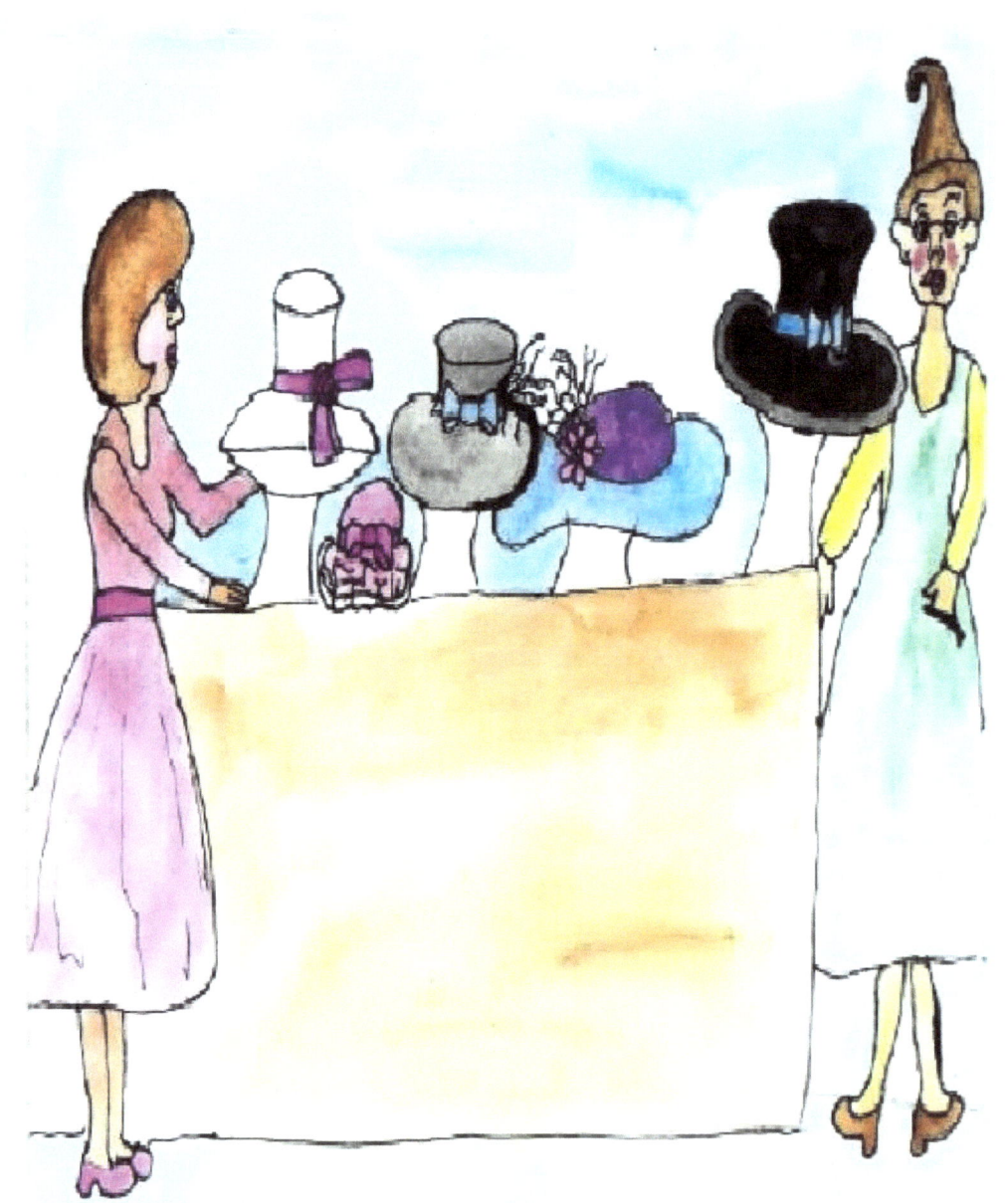

Mrs. Hubbard came over to the counter

To look at the new hats.

Helen asked if she had time for tea.

Mrs. Hubbard said. "I would love to but

I am running late my dear.

I will have my driver pick up the hats.

Pleas if you could have them boxed up

I'll have him come back in a half an hour.

Helen said that would be fine

Therefore Mrs. Hubbard left leaving

Miss. Pillbox behind.

(12)

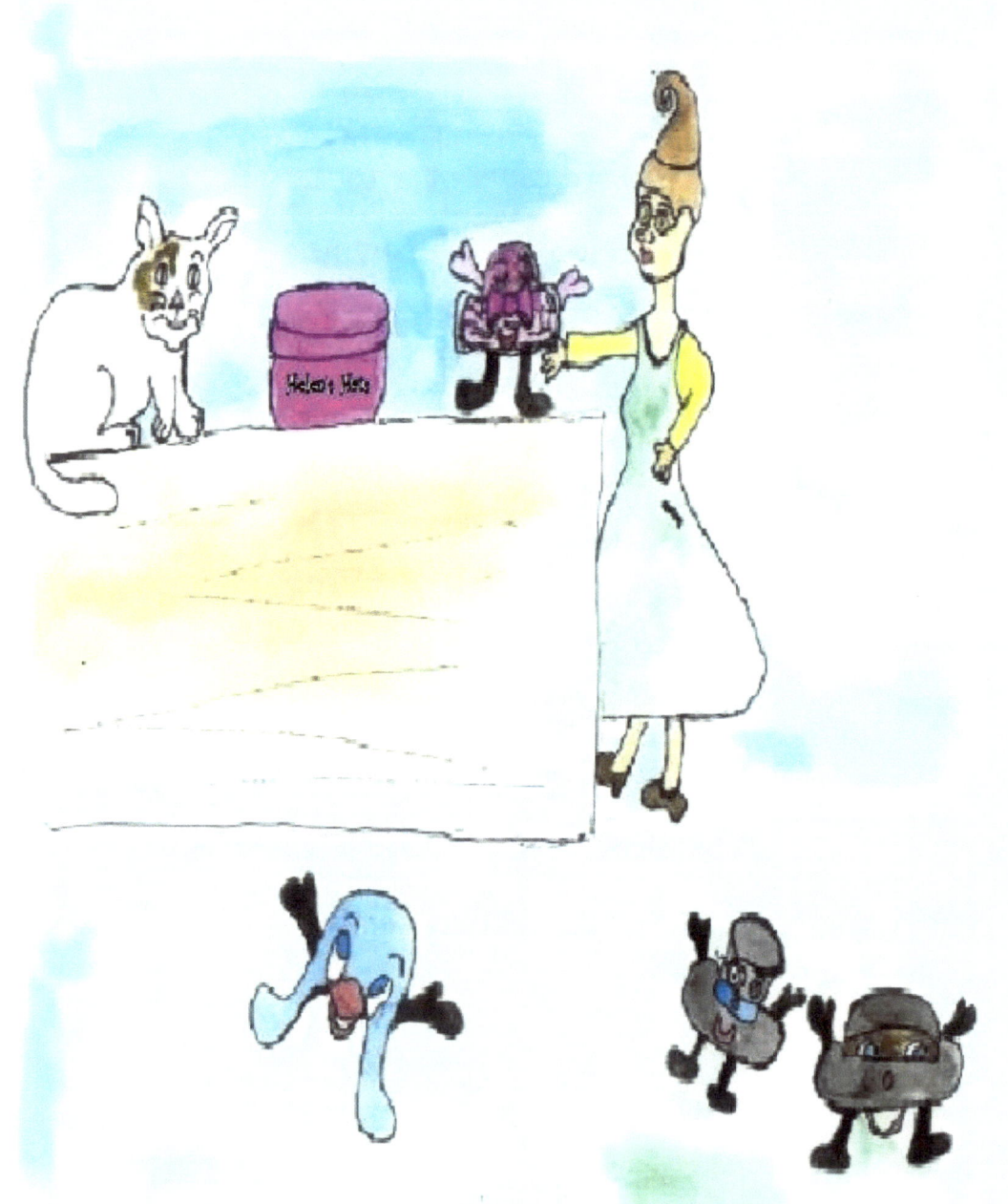

All the hats started laughing

Helen saw that Miss. Pillbox was on the counter

So she put her in a box.

Mr. Top hat and Miss. Cloche were not happy.

"Mary said, "Now, now you two

It well be all right you will see each

Other again in the shop".

(13)

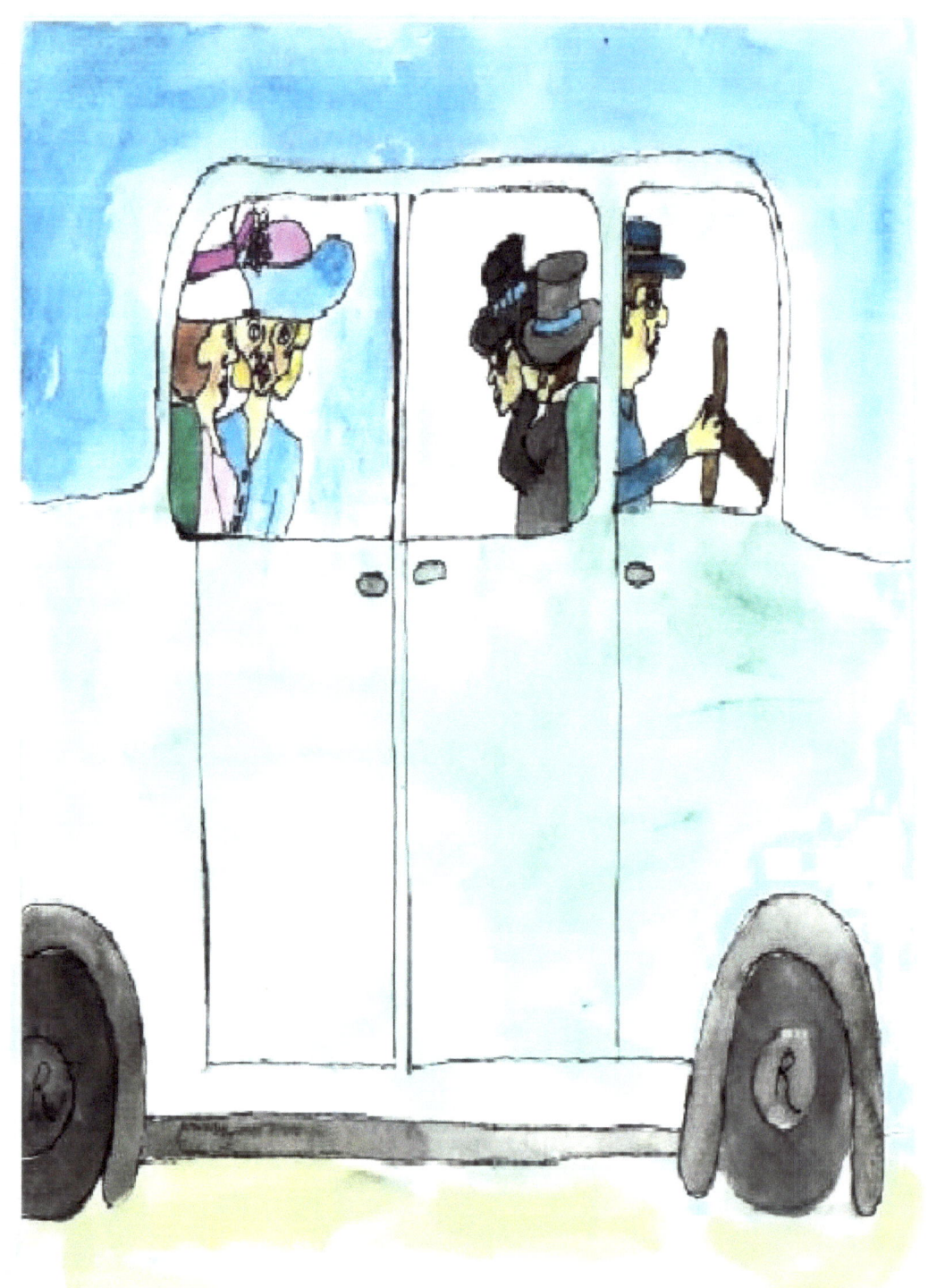

It was the day of the Derby.

Mrs. Hubbard and her family were all

Dressed up with their new hats on.

They all looked lovely.

It's was time so they got into the

Car and off they went to the Derby.

(14)

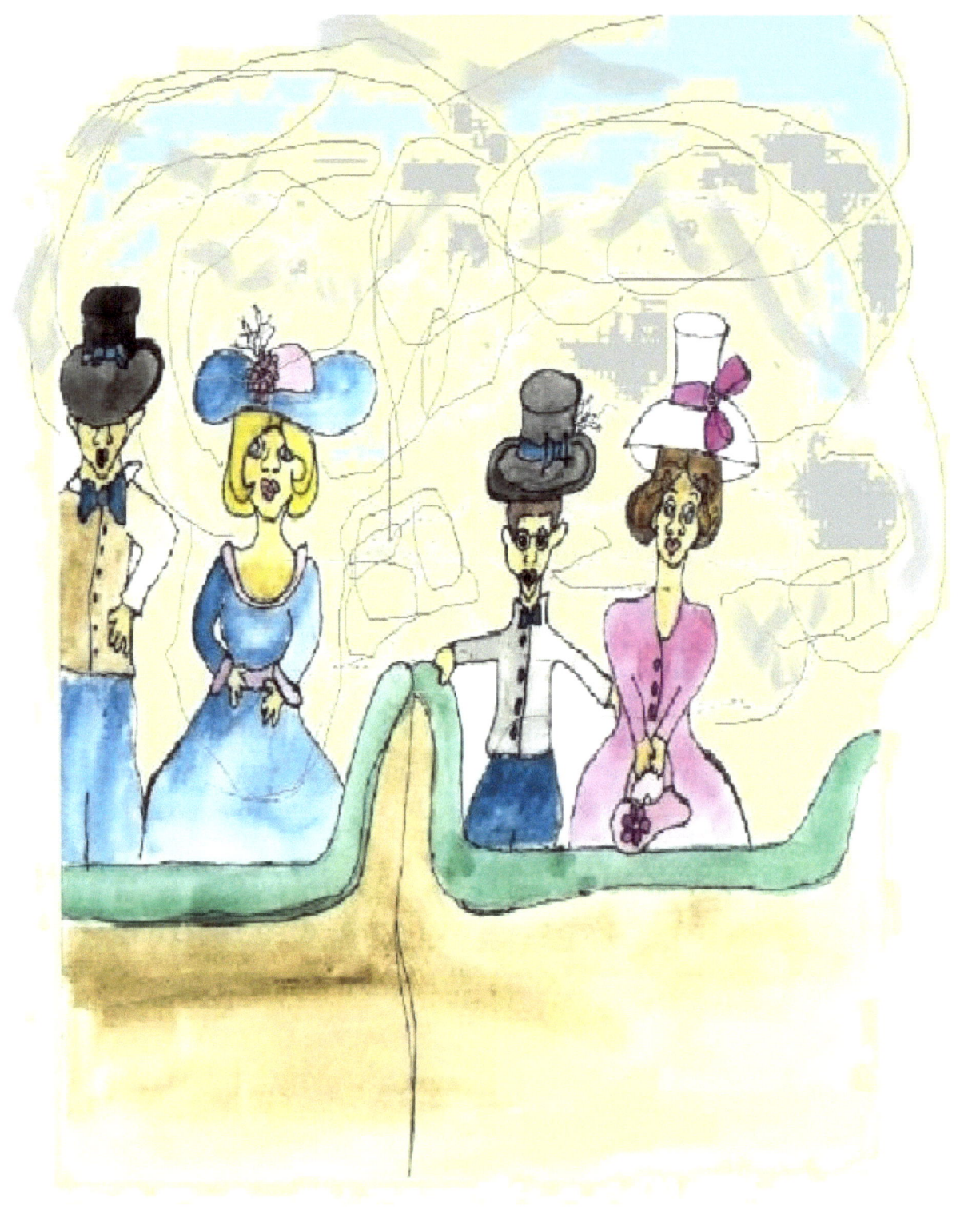

The Derby was crowded

The Hubbard family had front row seats.

They were enjoying the nice sunny day.

No rain was in sight

The first race was just starting when low and behold.

A big wind came up, it blow so hard all of the hat's in

Mrs. Hubbard Family blow away.

Off they went down to the track.

(15)

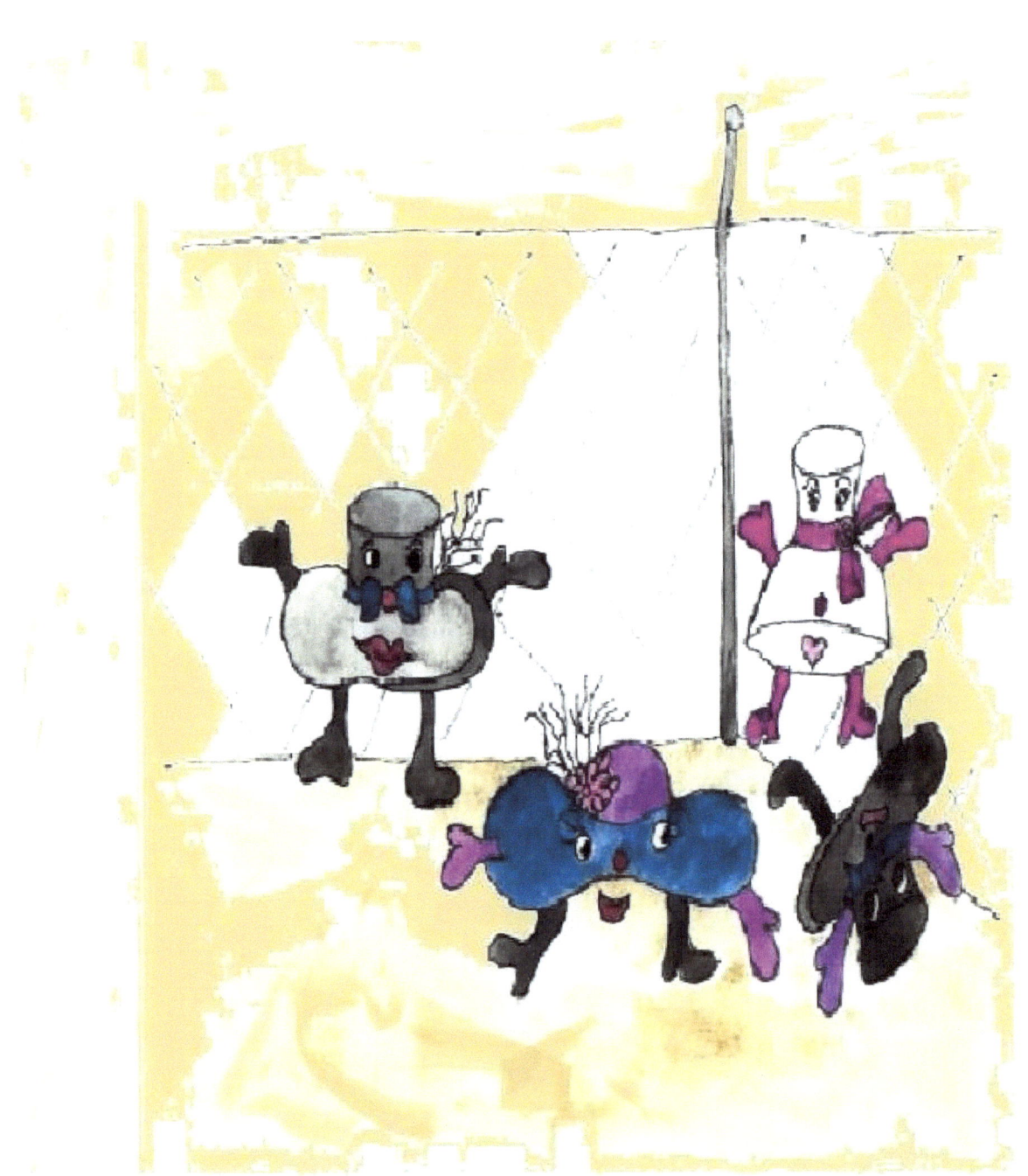

The Derby was over it was late in the day

And the crowed left. The hats that blow down to

The track they were up against a corner of the fence.

Later that night the hats came to life asking.

"Where are we?"

Mr. Hamburger said "I think we are on the racetrack."

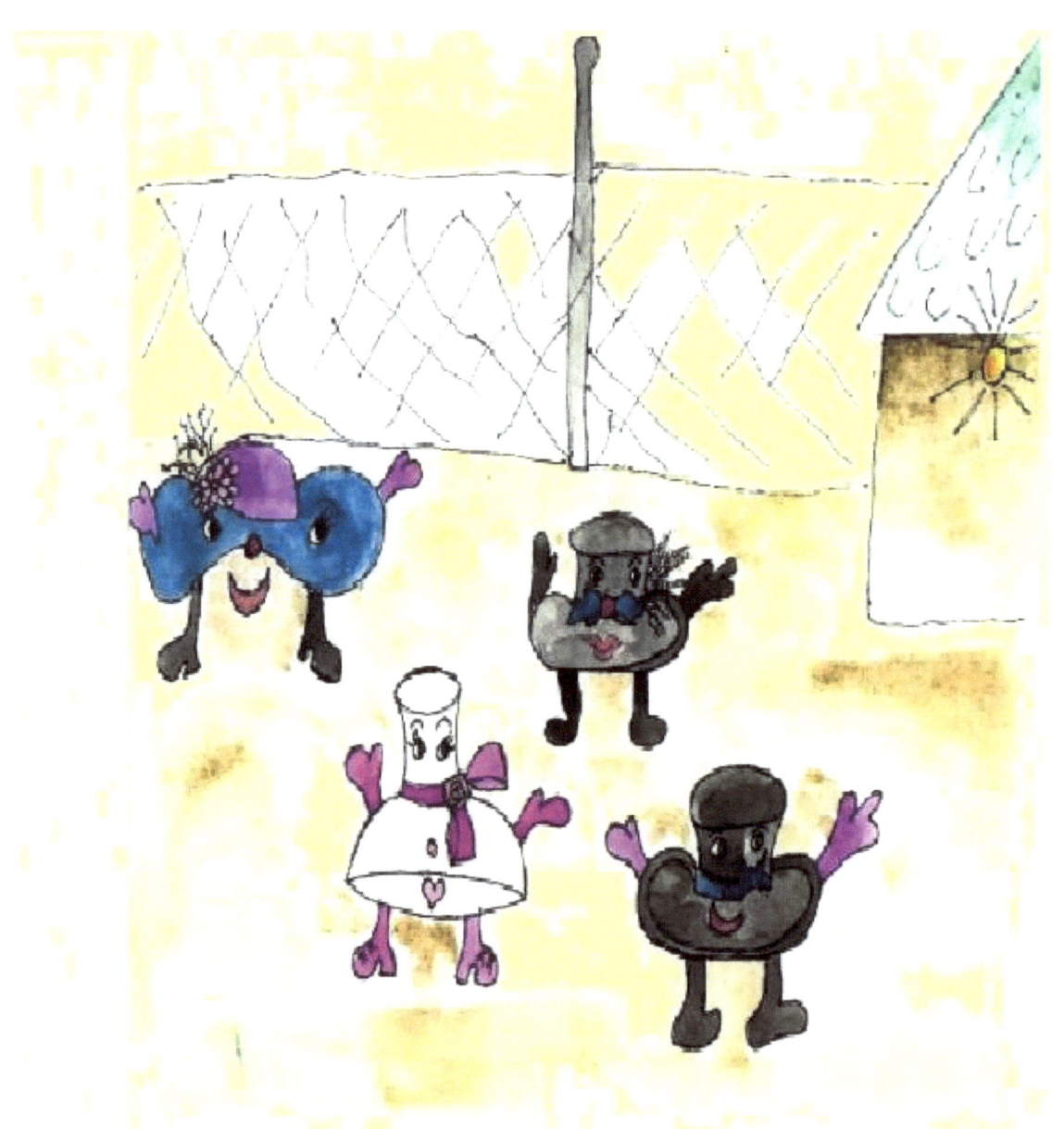

Missis said I'm scared and so was Miss. Church

The Boys told them not to worry.

"We will be alright". Mr. Jaxon said

"Come this way! There a light over this way".

So off they went towards the light. It was the

Light at the stable where the horse stayed it was there home.

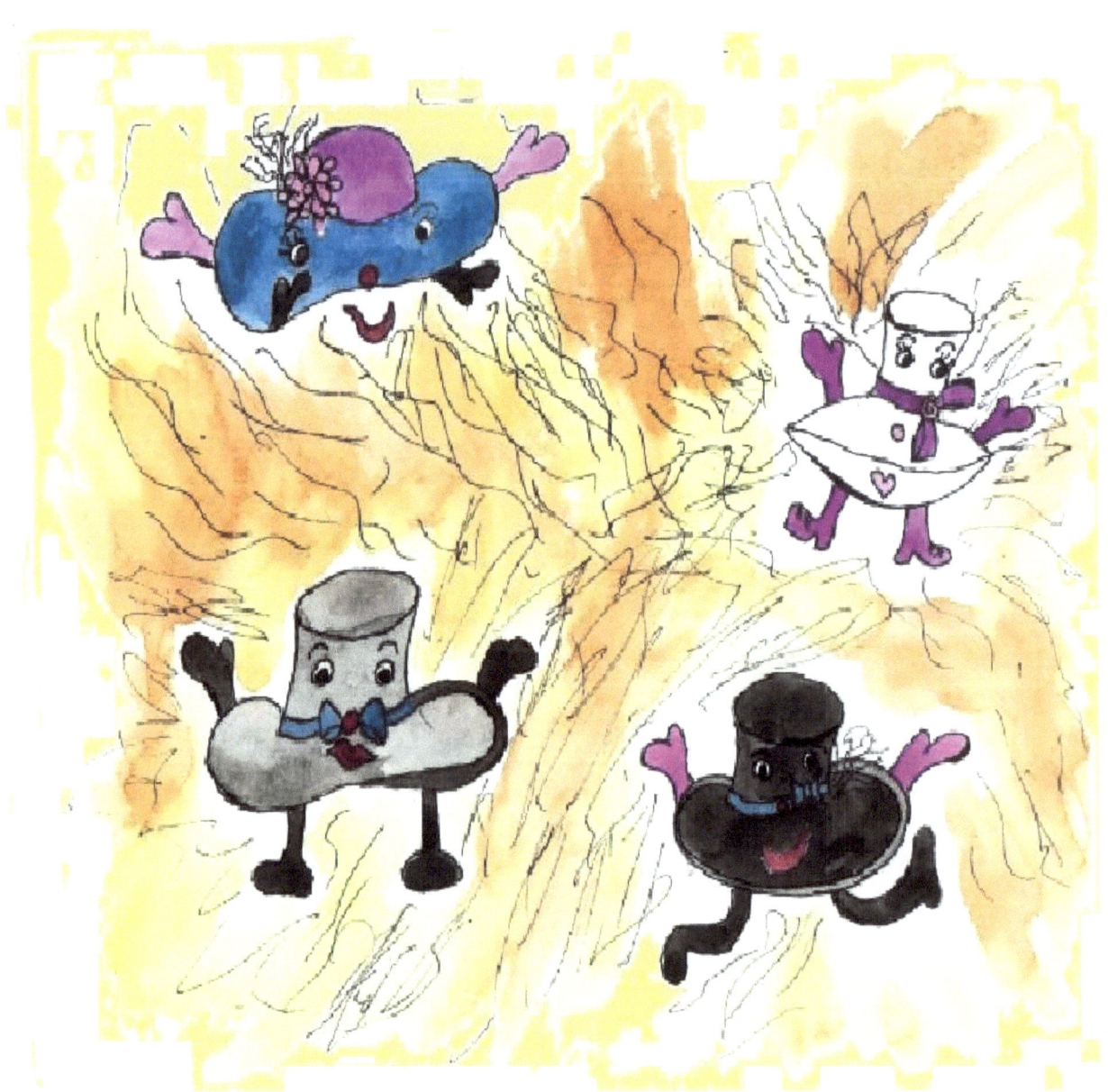

The hats went into the stables.

There was a pile of hay on one side of the stable.

Missis went over to it and the other hats fallowed her.

They all jumped into the soft, sweet smelling hay.

It was soft and smelled so good what fun they had!

(18)

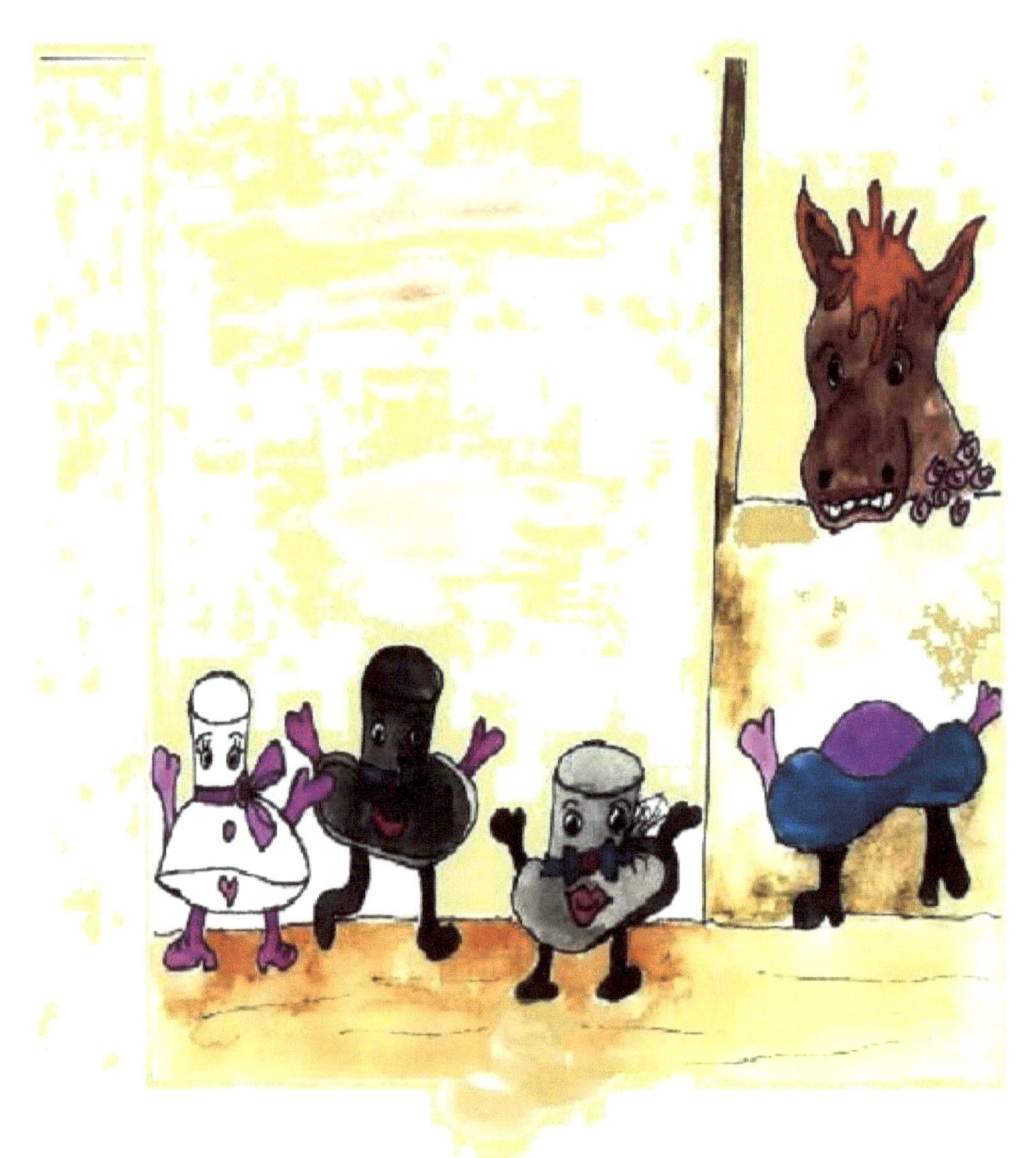

They left the hay and went over to a horse

Who was looking out of his stall at them?

He said "Hi you guy what's up?

All the hats laughed. We're just looking around".

Missis asked, what is your name? "The horse asked,"

"Have you ever ridden on a horse's back?"

"No but could you give us a ride

Back Home to Mrs. Hubbard's house Please.

(19)

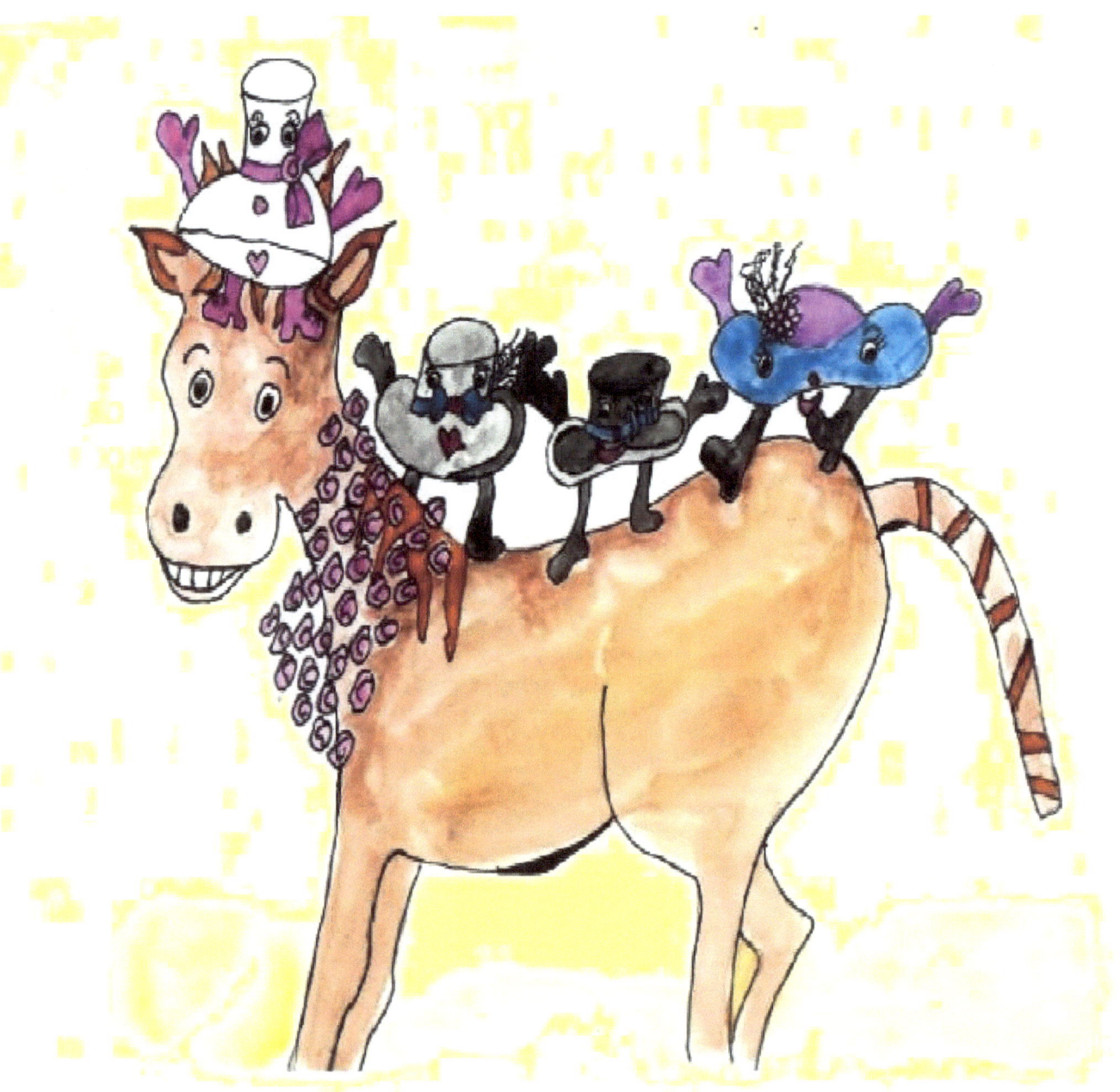

I'd love to then they all jump on Oliver's back for a ride.

The horse said up, up, I will tack you

All for a ride and then back home.

One of the hats jumped on his head

All the other on his back.

This was going to be fun!

(20)

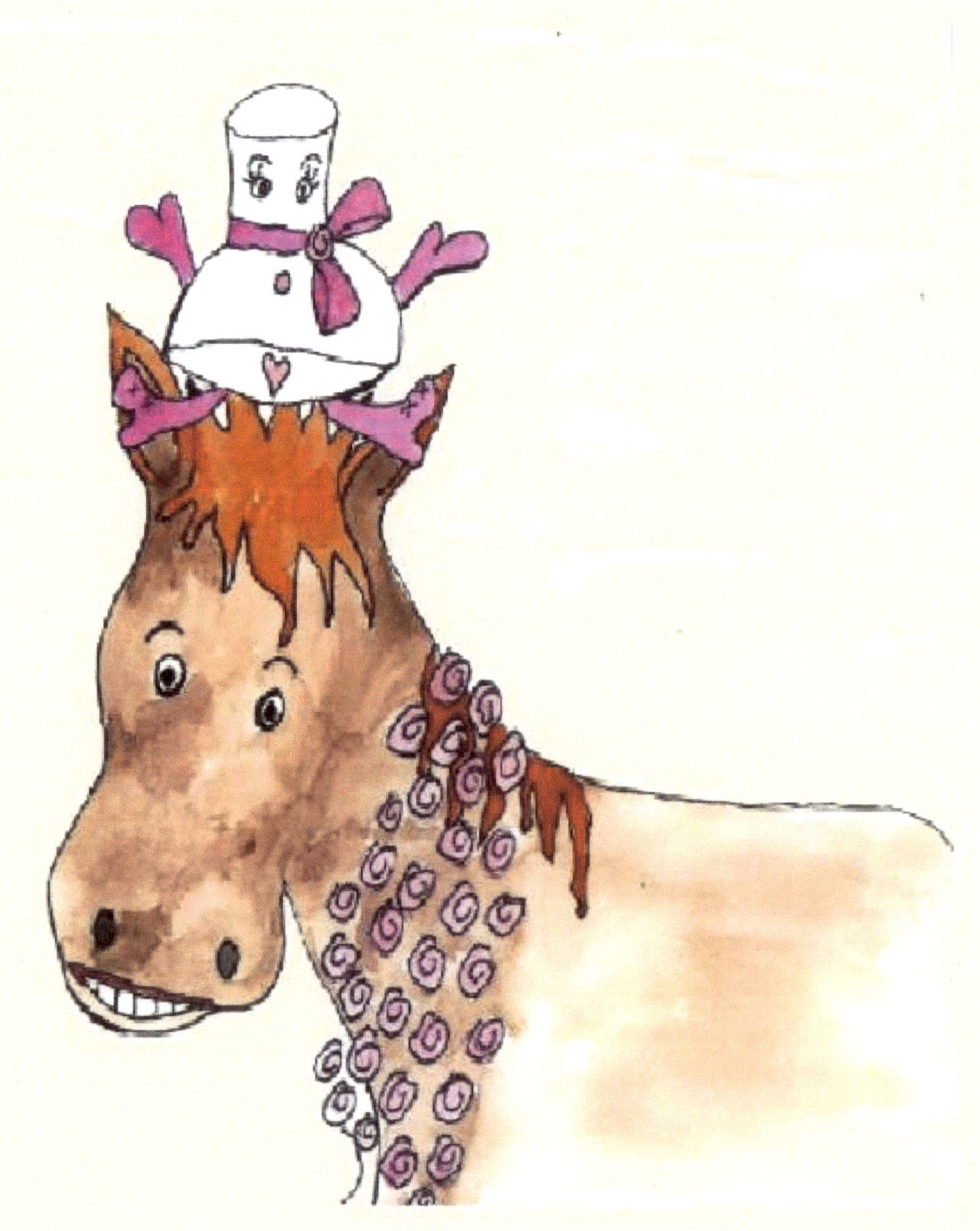

Oliver had a large garland of roses around his neck.

Miss. Church said you have the same kind of flowers around

"You neck that I have on my hat!" Oliver said

"Those are roses I was the winner of the race today".

"That why they put those on my neck to show off to

All the other horses". Miss. Church said I like them and thank you

Oliver for tacking us home you are a good horse.

(21)

The End

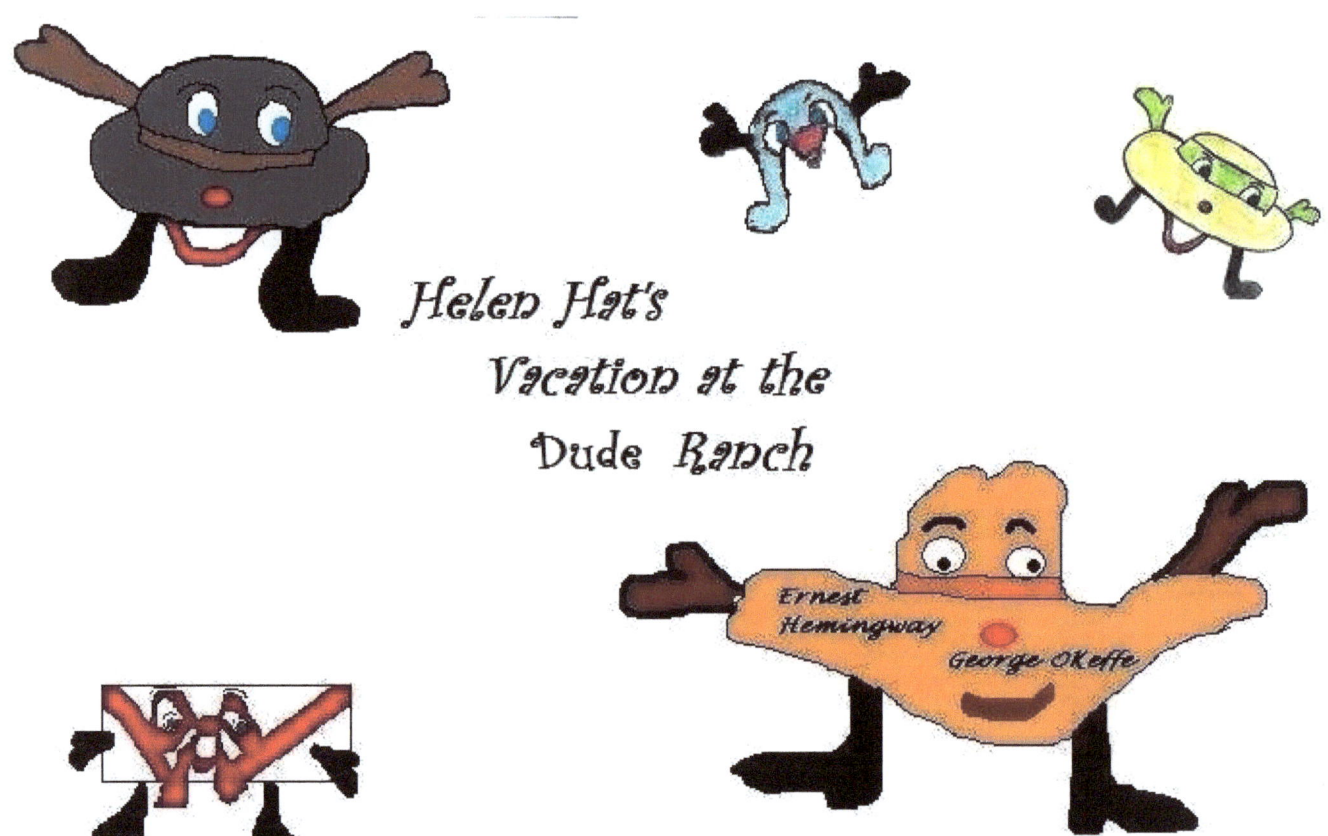

Helen Hat's
Vacation at the
Dude Ranch

Ernest Hemingway

George OKeffe

By Martha E Benzler